Who
in the hell
do you
Think
you are?

Denika Carothers

Who in the hell do you Think you are?

Are you the one responsible for screwing up your own life?

Denika Carothers

First Edition, February 2015

Copyright ©2015 Denika Penn-Carothers

For information contact denikacarothers@yahoo.com.

www.DenikaCarothers.com

Author/Publisher: Denika Carothers

Book cover design: Denika Carothers

ISBN 978-0-9886036-2-2

Acknowledgements

Even before I made a choice on which profession to venture into, I have literally spent my life wanting to help people to do and be their best selves. I believe that we are all created with a purpose and our destiny is dependent on how we choose to live our lives. The irony is that my greatest lessons came through my own life's challenges, of which there have been many. Because of those challenges and the subsequent lessons learned, I have been able to understand, help and motivate others. It's my life's passion and my life's work.

I can honestly say that I understand how each one of those challenges has designed, refined and created the individual that I am today, for which I am grateful – I absolutely love who I turned out to be!

Many people have been a part, and played a part in the journey of my life. The first beautiful and amazing example of love in my life was my mother, Anne Penn, who departed this earth in September 2011. By her example she taught me what unconditional love looks like. I know how to love because she was an amazing and positive teacher and force in my life.

My father, Frank Penn, who departed November 2009, was a living example to me of how hard work, persistence and following your calling and life purpose equates to a rewarding and peaceful experience. *"Even when people don't understand you it's important that you understand yourself"*, was one of the greatest lessons my father taught me through his example.

My children Antuan, Destiné and Annelea are, and have pretty much always been, a major blessing in my life. Not only am I their mother, but can say proudly that I have become one of their closest friends (by their confession at one time or another). They are the reason I have always done what I have because I want them to see, through my example, what it means to live a life of love, joy and authenticity.

These ladies have just recently come into my life but it feels like they've been there a long time. To my Master Mind sisters, Tanya, Felicia and Genyne, I want you to know that I appreciate your sisterhood, your friendship and your master minds. Thank you for your encouragement, through your belief in me, and your support in various ways of this completed work. You have inspired me to be greater as I watch the greatness in each one of you. Real sisterhood is something that every woman should have the opportunity to experience.

And last but not least my sister Daphne. You have helped me to understand and practice at a different level, what it means to relate in relationships. Thank you for allowing me to play this out with you in this lifetime, and thank you for always at the end of the day, being my sister.

Introduction

I cannot and I WILL not be defined. My greatness is not dependent on it being understood by others. My greatness lies in the acceptance of none other than myself.

My greatness does not depend on you and your greatness does not depend on me, but I can assure you that together we allow for, and bring forth, the greatness that is in each other.

My calling has come at a great price. I have experienced much pain, loss, heartache and disappointment in my life. However I realized a long time ago that to whom much is given much is required.

I have always been that person that everyone called upon for help, for strength, for guidance and for encouragement. It was always something that I willingly and lovingly stepped into being.

The challenge experienced when you are a strong person is, it seems when you have your weak moments there is nowhere to turn, because everyone is looking to you to strengthen them in one way or another.

When my only sister passed away in 1999, due to a car accident, I thought my heart was going to break. I never knew pain could feel that way. Although she was not the first person close to me that had passed away, at the time of her passing she was the closest person to me that had died. Words could not explain what I was feeling when I was going through that experience.

I quickly realized after her passing, as a matter of fact it was actually the next day, that in spite of what is going on around you, you still have the choice to live your life. You can choose to see the 'good' or you can choose to let the 'bad' pull you under and suffocate you until you yourself, feel like you are going to die.

I made a conscious choice in that experience that I would focus more on being grateful that I had her as my sister for 29 years, than focus on the heartache that was very real for me every morning when I awoke. She was a gift to me; she was my baby sister and we had an amazing relationship and friendship.

My acceptance of this "it is what it is, and it will be what it will be" moment, ushered me into the ability to have compassion such as I had never known before. It ushered me into realizing that there was a "bigger picture" to this experience called life, and it ushered me into a determination that I would fulfill the reason, without hesitation or complaint, for why I was here on this earth.

May your journey of life be one that you will look back on one day and say, **"The life that I lived was created by me -- I participated in it** fully and lovingly, and I enjoyed every minute of it!"

Here's to your joy, your peace and your purpose.

In love and light…..Denika

Foreward

A bright light!

After speaking with Denika on the phone I knew she was a force to be reckoned with immediately. Then after meeting her for the first time in person, I knew my life wouldn't be the same. Denika's gift was glaringly apparent from the moment I encountered her. Insightfulness, intuitiveness, honesty, bravery, trustworthiness and faith-filled, all wrapped in love, is what she brought to me each time I was in her presence. Even over the phone every bit of that came through before I even laid eyes on her.

She has unapologetically called me out on my own contribution to what I'm seeing in my life. She lovingly does not let me off the hook when I want to have a pity party, or dwell on the past, or not take responsibility for what I'm creating with the thoughts I allow and the words I choose to speak.

This notion of taking responsibility completely for what a person sees in their own life is very challenging. Denika has demonstrated many times over that she is fully present and able to help you see what you need to know that you don't already know. In other words, she is able to help you see your blind spots and facilitates awareness of how you affect what is showing up in your life. The work that she does is important and amazingly transformative. I am very appreciative that our paths have crossed.

This book should be in every person's hand that wants to recreate their life. She gives practical and sound guidance on how to experience the life that supports your Highest Self. This body of work is really a step by step instructional guide that will lead you down a path of balance, joy and peace, and will show you how to successfully create and achieve your greatest life.

Denika is a bright powerful light that showed up in my life for sure!

Genyne Vinson

Denika Carothers

Contents

Denika Carothers

ONE

You ARE What You Think

Scripture states, "As a man thinks in his heart, he is." You are what you think and what you think, you are.

So who do you think you are? Most people identify who they are as the roles that they play, for example, a mother, a father, a banker, a lawyer, etc. Often finding out who we are begins with discovering who we are not. So let's cover that first. You are not:

- Your gender
- Your nationality or ethnicity
- Your ego
- Your persona
- Your family situation

1

- Your profession
- Your emotions
- Your history

You are not your role or your labels. It is important to understand that we are all Spiritual beings having a human experience.

"*We can only be who we are and at some point that has to be good enough.*" - Panache Desai

Who we identify ourselves as being is another area where we allow the world and others to De-Fine us. So many people are criticized, physically, emotionally and mentally abused, with very little good being said about them as children. Because of this they identify who they are with more negative, than they do positive.

We can become products of our environment but at some point, when you no longer feel good about who you 'think' you are, it's time to make a decision to make some changes.

The hardest part of taking any first step is to make the decision to do so. Once we decide within ourselves to DO something we usually put the action behind the decision. I come across people all the time in my practice whose major complaint is, *"I just don't know HOW to do it."*

My reply to this is always, *"You do it by making a decision to do so. Will you make the commitment to make the decision?"*

Changing your thoughts takes no more effort than changing your diet, changing your job or changing your relationships. The first step to doing any of these is to make the decision to do so. But the truth is that people are lazy, indecisive and complacent, and so they choose to remain in their very uncomfortable "comfort zones."

Even though we have labeled them "comfort zones" most people will admit that they don't feel very comfortable in these spaces. So what motivates people to stay where they don't want to be? The fear of change, being too lazy to do anything, or choosing to settle for less than they believe they deserve.

Knowing who you are leads to an experience of living a life that is harmonized and full of meaning. Discovering who you are allows you to be grounded in your authentic self, or what I like to call your Beingness, or your essence. When you connect with the essence of **who** you are you feel supported in making choices and decisions that are in alignment with your "Highest Self." You can then begin to create your life by design rather than living by default.

Discovering your "true self" and learning how to respond to life in light of this insight and wisdom, can be a great challenge. The first thing you need to do is discern what your authentic self is and separate it from all the false identities that yourself, and others, have labeled you with.

Our identities often take the form of old habits of mind that have been accrued over our life time in reaction to difficulty, disappointments and uncertainty. Having had to endure a constant stream of criticism as a child, may have caused you to believe that you are not worthy, that you are incapable or you see yourself as a failure. These are examples of thoughts that when left unmanaged and continually entertained can result in us *being* the thing that we think about our self.

A skillful way to begin to understand who you are is to examine those aspects of yourself that you have mistakenly believed were the real you. Understand that your emotions are reflections of mind states and because they can be released they don't define who you are.

Your history does not define you. It is simply an accumulation of actions and events that characterize you at a particular moment in your life. It does not define your essence. Though you may not have had a choice concerning your history, you can choose how you *respond* to it. Developing the capacity to do this will lead you to a deeper relationship with your authentic self, and a more genuine experience of life.

Your identity is not the sum of your habits, duties and/or responsibilities. You may as a child have had to take on major responsibilities which you did not like, but now feel that who you are is created around being 'responsible'. Because of this you may find it hard *not* to "take on" responsibilities.

When you mistake your habits and responsibilities for your essence, you close yourself off from feelings of authenticity. This is one of the main reasons why mothers struggle with their sense of self when their children leave home. They have identified themselves by their roles and so do not know who they are without the "responsibility" of taking care of their children.

Your persona is that aspect of yourself that you present to the public. How many people in a public setting become totally different than they are in private? Many do. Personality traits are like software that you interface with your life. Even though a public face may be deemed necessary in social settings, because it has the capacity to change it does not define your "true self."

When you can begin to put distance between your inner and your outer identity your sense of authenticity increases, because you are not controlled by the fear of your persona being exposed or diminished.

Now for many the aspect of themselves that they identify most with is their egoic nature. I like to describe the ego as a committee composed of characters with different agendas and points of view. Recognizing this committee in your mind can be dismaying and liberating; dismaying because you lose the false security of having a fixed mind, and

7

liberating because you now know that you don't have to believe your thoughts.

Each person's thinking and core identity is determined by, and is a reflection of, conditions of heart. "As, a man thinketh in his heart", so will he become.

My personal "I AM" revelation completely and profoundly altered my thinking process. Several years ago while having a meeting with a gentleman who had come in from the island of Jamaica, I was asked by said gentleman this question:

"Who are you?"

I was stumped. I didn't know how to answer this question. So I immediately sought the answer from within through prayer by asking silently: *"who am I?"*

The answer that I received took me aback and initially I didn't quite know how to interpret it.

I heard these words. *"You are the incarnated being of God, you are God incarnate."*

Well I immediately knew that this wasn't me speaking to me because I didn't talk like this. *"The incarnated being of God"*, I thought, *"What was that?"* My first thought was that it sounded kind of blasphemous. So I spoke that thought silently within myself and immediately the same words were repeated back to me, but stronger this time.

I had come to understand by this time when Spirit was communicating with me, and so I repeated the words that had been spoken to me to the gentleman. His response to me was, *"And don't you ever forget it!"*

This was a life-changing experience for me. I realized in that moment that I was so much greater than what I thought of myself. You see for many years I wrestled with self-esteem and self-worth issues. The funny and ironic thing though is that people always saw the gift in me, but I could not see it in myself. My vision of my true nature had been obscured by the opinions, confessions, beliefs and criticisms of others about and towards me. Those words had been stored in my subconscious and even though I knew for a long time that I had been called to be greater and achieve more, I couldn't achieve greater because my thoughts were more in alignment with fear of failure, lack of confidence, and the fear of being judged and rejected.

But these words spoken to my spirit by Spirit, took me to another place… a place of strength, a place of purpose, and a place of greatness. I thought, *"If I am the incarnated being of God, and God incarnate, then that means, like God, I have the power to be, do and have whatever I can think."* Since that day my set intention is to align my thoughts with the higher calling of my purpose; that come what may I will achieve the greatness to which I was called. Are you ready to achieve the greatness to which you have been called? Then keep reading…

> "If every morning
>
> You can find a reason to say,
>
> "Yes, it's going to be a beautiful day."
>
> And every day, you find a reason to say,
>
> "Yes, it is a beautiful day."
>
> And every night you find a reason to say,
>
> "Yes, it was a beautiful day."
>
> Then one day,
>
> You'll look back and easily say,
>
> "Yes... it was a beautiful life."
>
> *Unknown*

Denika Carothers

TWO

Get Out of Your Head

When you are born you start with an empty slate... you come in to the world Fine! There is no predefined identity, no character and no personality. NOTHING! Then life begins and it brings along with it experiences, thoughts, understandings, and conditionings. The world begins to De-Fine us. You begin to develop beliefs that are a result of your thoughts. Then you begin to develop truths which are a result of your beliefs.

Our beliefs, which then turn into our truths, come from three places... experiences, cultures and conditioning. Every thought that you have about the world, and yourself, up until the time that you can think for yourself, come from your world and the people around you.

Have you ever asked yourself any of these questions…

"Why do I think what I think?"

"Why do I believe what I believe?"

"Is what I think the way it really is?"

"Is what I believe the truth?"

When you make a decision that it's time to get out of your own head, I recommend that you start with these questions.

The scriptures tell us that "as a man thinks *in his heart* so he is." Does this mean that every thought that we think in our head about our self is not who we really are? Hmmm, something to ponder on, but one thing that I have proven is that the thoughts that we think in our head, when internalized and believed in our heart, create our experiences, our realities and our truths.

I have learned the importance of getting out of *my* head. This came about when I began to question EVERYTHING that I *thought* to be true. I decided that if what I thought was really the truth then I should not be afraid to question it. The truth will stand as truth, even after it is questioned. The truth does not need defending.

The challenge for many people is they don't know why they believe what they do. They secretly question *what* they believe and yet are afraid that if they question it, they will shake the very foundation of all they know to be 'true'. But isn't that crazy? If what you believe is not the truth, why on earth would you not want to question it and give yourself the opportunity to discover the real truth?

When you discover that *your* truths, beliefs and thoughts are not in alignment with what is actually true, then it is time to make a decision. You can choose to Re-Fine yourself or you can make the choice to allow the conditioning of the world to continue to De-Fine you.

Most people are afraid of change, but change occurs every minute of every day. The body that you now walk around in has changed over and repeatedly; it is not the same body that you came to this earth in. As a matter of fact it has continually changed since the day of your birth and will continue to change until the time you depart from this earth. Change is inevitable.

To discover who you truly are you have to be willing to get out of your head and connect with your heart. For it is in your heart that the true nature and essence of who you are abides. The mouth does not always speak the truth however the heart always contains the truth.

Do you know what the first part that forms in the human body is? How many of you said the brain? No it's not the brain. The first organ that forms in the human body is the heart. The heart is the nucleus of the human body but more people focus on what is going on inside of the head, or the mind.

"All of our behavior results from the thoughts that preceded it. So the thing to work on is not your behavior but the thing that caused your behavior, your thoughts." - **Dr. Wayne Dyer**

Within the ability of our creativity perspectives we can see our thoughts as the way our mind characterizes, describes or explains the energy that our body perceives. Our mind's ability to characterize is connected to our past experiences and how we have focused our attention and awareness. Whether we experience this as an image, an idea, a vision or an awareness of knowing something does not matter. The process of thought is simply our mind 'playing' with the energy we experience. In this regard thoughts are simply consciousness at play with the energy that consciousness experiences.

From the perspective of creativity, human beings have been wired with the ability to create. Everything that was created began as a thought and was subsequently converted into an action. We have the ability through our thought processes to take formless energy and create form.

This is why learning how to be *intentional* in your thinking is extremely important. I like to call this process Conscious Thinking. We create our realities by way of our thoughts. Our realities are created by way of our perceptions and it is important to understand that we participate 100% in the outcomes of our situations, circumstances and experiences.

There is an analogy that is often made between the human mind and the computer. The mind is said to be a kind of super-computer, greater, better and more efficient than any computer there is. And like a computer the mind can be programmed to perform many different behaviors; both the computer and the mind store files and programs in their memory (or subconscious) until they are needed.

In computers these programs are those that let you write documents such as letters, reports or books like this one. The computer also allows us to surf the internet, play music, videos and much more. By analogy programs stored in the human mind allow us to know how to ride a bike, play the piano, sing and dance, cook or drive a car. The human subconscious stores programs such as rejection, disappointment, hurt, grief, joy and belief systems.

Once a thought or memory has been programmed, it is stored in our subconscious and can be recalled at any time. This is why we have reactions to things when a 'trigger' is pressed or a 'nerve' is touched, bringing to the surface an emotion or response that causes us discomfort.

We may have been criticized as a child, and the moment someone does something that subconsciously reminds us of the pain, or discomfort of that memory, we react. Or we were mistreated by a past lover and even though we are now in a loving and wonderful relationship, one incident, word or action can be the trigger or nerve that sends us right back to the memory and causes us to react from that discomfort or pain. This is why many people find themselves experiencing cyclical patterns over and over again even though the past relationship has been long left.

This is when it becomes necessary to confront the thoughts in your head and ask the question, *"is this thought or way of thinking continuing to serve me or is it time to let this go?"* The reason why this is so important is because if you don't do something different, you will experience the same things over and over again. Remember, "as a man thinks in his heart so he is." What you focus on you draw to yourself and what you think, you are! This is when you have to make the decision to get out of your head especially if your head is the place that you need to get away from.

You may realize that this is something you need to do but your question is, *"how do I get out of my head?"* The answer… by making a decision to do so! It really is that simple and that's the first step.

"*All of our Knowledge has its origins in our Perceptions.*"

Leonardo De Vinci

THREE

What You Focus On, Expands

There are absolutes that I know to be true in life. What you focus on expands, is one of those truths. Another way of saying this is, "where attention goes energy flows." - James Redfield

For me personally it has become a focus of intention to align my thoughts only with what I want to be reflected in my experiences. I have learned that what you expect, you experience. In my practice I often hear these words from clients… "struggle", "hard", "difficult", "awful" "stressful" "I can't", and do you know what their lives are? Stressful, a struggle, hard, difficult, awful, and they find that they can't do what they desire to do. Their life reflects back to them the things that they are focusing on. What we focus on we draw to ourselves over and over again. Like energy attracts like energy or as the scriptures put it, "like attracts like."

"Any habit or pattern whether we call it "good" or "bad", despite our best intentions, tends to reassert itself over time unless we break that pattern by doing something different." - **Dan Millman**

For a person to successfully make a shift from this way of thinking, they have to be prepared to recognize the negative thought that results in the negative confession, or spoken words. And once recognized, the need to shift and release the resistance to change, becomes necessary.

One of my favorite quotes from the late Maya Angelou is **"when you know better, you do better."** When you *learn* better but you choose to continue to make choices that are not in alignment with your highest good, and think the same negative thoughts over and over again, you then assume full responsibility, whether knowingly or unknowingly, for your experienced outcomes.

So let me break this down a little further for you as to what this really means.

- When you focus on not having money, you expand being broke.

- When you focus on problems in the relationship, you expand being in a broken relationship.

- When you focus on stress, you expand anxiety.

- When you focus on not being good enough, you expand failure.

- When you focus on hating your job, you expand opposition in the workplace.

When you focus on something the Universe replies, "Your wish is my command!" We must ask ourselves often *"What am I focusing on?"* If you discover that it's something negative then you must change it to something that is in alignment with what you want to experience. Let your focus be on something positive, something you would like to experience. Remember your thoughts create your realities, your situations and your circumstances; the more you focus on a negative situation, the more of it you will create for yourself. But the good news is this... the more you focus on a positive situation the more of *it* you create for yourself.

So how can you change a negative focus to a positive one? Well let's use an example that many people can relate to. Let's say we have been focusing on not having enough money and on having too many bills, and feel that we are so far under that we may never catch up. As you will be able to see in your circumstances, the more you think about not having enough the more you create financial hardship and stress. We can change the outcome by changing our focus in this way:

1. **Begin to focus** on, "how can I create more money in my life?"

2. **Decide to respect the money** you do have. You can practice this first by taking the time to organize the money in your wallet or purse, instead of just throwing it around. Organize it into denominations and face all bills in the same direction. Remember what you dishonor you turn away.

3. **When you see money** on the streets or sidewalks, even if it is a penny, if it is in your reach pick it up and say thank you to the Universe for sending you money. Bless it and visualize it multiplying 1000 times or more.

4. **If you have a change drawer** or jar, you can organize those coins and turn them into bills.

Many grocery stores have machines that will help you do this.

5. **Use what you have paid for**. If you are not using it sell it or give it away and bless someone with it. This will make room for more to come your way. As you release things you open a doorway for more good to come in to your life.

Change your focus and you will change your circumstances.

"Our minds become magnetized with the dominating thoughts we hold in our minds and these magnets attract to us the forces, the people, the circumstances of life which harmonize with the nature of our dominating thoughts." - **Napoleon Hill**

Remember your thoughts are powerful, powerful things! Your focus puts your subconscious mind to work and it stays busy finding more and more of what you are focused on. Keep this in mind and focus on what you **do** want, what's right for you, and how you want things to work in your favor. Consistently be aware of your thoughts and if you find yourself focusing on something that you do not desire to create, or experience, simply change the thought quickly. This will help you to become a conscious creator. This works... I promise!

"The more you

Praise and Celebrate

Your Life,

The more

there is in life

To Celebrate."

Oprah Winfrey

FOUR

The Man in the Mirror – Friend or Foe?

Okay so in the beginning of your life the power to define you was left up to others. But now, at this juncture, who are you allowing to De-Fine you? And, if you have taken over the job of defining yourself, when you look at yourself in the mirror what do you tell yourself about yourself?

It is bad enough when people don't understand who we are and are not very kind in their definition of us, but when we are the one who is unkind to our own self, how great that unkindness tends to be.

When you look at yourself in the mirror what do you see? Who do you see? Do you criticize yourself or do you compliment yourself? Do you

31

see the things that you wish were *not* there, or are you grateful that the things you can see are there?

"The image that concerns most people is the reflection they see in other people's minds." – **Edward De Bono**

In a recent Dove ad an FBI forensic artist sketched a series of women based purely on the way they described themselves, and again sketched the women as others had described them. The artist could only hear the voices of these women; he could not see their faces.

A video about the experiment which has been viewed on YouTube more than 65 million times and counting, revealed the stark difference between how these women viewed themselves when compared to how others saw them. Across the board, the way the women described *themselves* were the least attractive, suggesting, according to the Dove marketing team, that we are all more beautiful than we *think* we are.

So why can't we see ourselves as we really are?

This was a major challenge for me for a very long time. Whenever I would look at myself in the mirror all I did was highlight and focus on what was wrong – what was too fat, what was scarred, the lumps, the bumps and the imperfections.

By and large the negative view that I had of myself was because of what was transferred on to me as a child by other children, and to a great degree by my father. My weight and body image was the primary source of my insecurity. I was called fat by children in school. My father was always talking about my weight and "bribing" me to lose it. He would tell me what he would give me or buy me if I lost the weight.

Over the course of our lives, experts say our sense of self-image develops through a complicated interplay between cultural ideas, life experiences and accumulated comments by others. The result is inevitably, a distortion of reality.

All of our experiences, the teasing we go through as a child, all the self-consciousness we hold as teenagers, and all the worrying about whether we would be accepted as good enough, or attractive enough, are called forth in how people see and think of themselves. It's a combination of emotion, meaning and experience that builds up over our lifetime.

A great part of how we define ourselves and others, relates to body image. Among women the practice of criticizing the size and shape of their bodies, together with their friends, is a widespread phenomenon. This is especially true within certain demographics. In a study, that was conducted by Renee Engeln and her colleague R.H. Salk, it was discovered that when women heard "fat talk" they were more likely to engage in the conversation because they were dissatisfied with their body image, even though women who did the most fat talk did not weigh the most, and most of the women in the study were of average weight.

We know where it comes from and even though we feel most uncomfortable when we are the recipients of this kind of negative talk from outside of ourselves, we continue to perpetrate this same communication against ourselves, more often than not on a daily basis. Most people when they look at themselves in the mirror find something to criticize, rather than something to compliment.

The personal turn-around for me in this area came after I said a prayer of request asking God/Spirit/Source to allow me to see myself the way that I was seen by my Creator. After saying this prayer I set the intention to start appreciating the good aspects of myself, rather than what I saw as not so good. I began to have an attitude of gratitude regarding what I did have like eyes that could see, a stomach that did not have digestive disorders, legs that could walk and breasts that were cancer free, rather than focusing on beady eyes, a not so flat stomach, cellulite and large breasts.

I will tell you that an attitude of gratitude is the best anecdote for a negative mindset. When you focus on things for which you have to be grateful you begin to focus less on the things that you don't like, or don't have; the result of an appreciation for what you do have, is ever present.

So my recommendation is to make a decision to see what is good, what is lovely and what is praise-worthy about yourself, because the more you are able to visualize the good, the beautiful, and the blessings, the more of these you will welcome and usher into your life. Remember… thoughts become words and words become things.

"No problem can

be solved,

From the same

Level of

Consciousness

That created it."

Albert Einstein

Denika Carothers

FIVE

To Thine Own Self Be True

I believe that the reason you were drawn to this book is because on a subconscious level, and maybe even on a conscious level, you have made a decision to get back in touch with the real you, your "true self."

You know that you are not here on this earth by chance or coincidence. You know that you have a purpose for being here and you are now ready to step into that purpose. In order for you to know where you are going you have to first know *who's* going there. In order to be identified you have to have an identity and my intention is to help you to identify your "true self," the self that the Creator God intended you to be when you were created.

Take five minutes in silence before continuing

39

to read. Close your eyes and listen to yourself breathe as you ask yourself this question… ***"Who am I today?"*** Think of every word that you would use to describe who you believe yourself to be right now, the self that you interact with on a daily basis. Don't think about how others view you or how others would describe you. All that matters right now in this moment is how you see yourself. Go ahead close your eyes and describe you to yourself.

Now I'm going to ask you to have a truth moment. The person that you just described, is that the person that you believe you were created to be? Is that the REAL you or was that described person created by the circumstances and/or experiences of your life?

Were you abused and as a result of that abuse you decided that you need to be an angry person, who will never again allow anyone to get close enough to you to hurt you? Were you abandoned and as a result of that abandonment you closed off your feelings, shut your heart down and decided that you would never love anyone again? Were you rejected and because of it you made a decision that you will do everything within your power to protect yourself because you can't trust anyone else to be there for you?

What event or events contributed to you being the person that has been looking back at you in the mirror? Is that the true authentic you, the perfect being that God created you to be, or is that person the creation of the experiences, circumstances and conditioning of the world and others?

If you are willing to be open, allow me to walk this journey of self truth with you and help you to connect to your authentic self.

So who are you? I believe that it is important to acknowledge that you are a Spiritual being having a human experience. It is further my belief that we were all created by a Supreme Being who I refer to as God, the Almighty, Source, Spirit, The Divine. When we incarnate, are born into this earthly experience, we come to this life in our true essence. However the processes of life and the many different experiences that we encounter as we grow and move through life have a tendency to alter and mask the true nature of who we really are. We come into this world Fine, then the world De-Fines us and then we have to Re-Fine ourselves.

In so many instances we allow the challenges of life to steal away our true identities. In the process of discovering our true self and moving forward in our created purpose, being honest with oneself is an important first step. Being honest with others, while very important, is not as crucial as being honest with your own self. It is vital to your progression and growth. And the truth is that you can't really be honest with others if you have not learned how to be honest with yourself.

The true essence of our being never goes

away. In spite of how we may try to be someone we were not created to be, in spite of us having an intention to make choices that are not in alignment with our highest good, there is always a greater force at work in our lives.

Very few people are fully authentic all of the time in their outer expression. Most people feel a need to put on an act to get by. That's probably where the saying, "Fake it till you make it" came from. I really do not align with this quote! But some people spend more time living unauthentic lives than they spend being true to themselves.

It is unpleasant and damaging to us if we are trapped in jobs or relationships where we rarely get the chance to be ourselves. If we indeed feel trapped, whether in a job, a relationship or any other situation, we need to make an effort to change our circumstances as soon as possible so we can be free to express ourselves authentically.

Being dishonest with yourself is like placing your own self in a cage and locking the door. Even more damaging is when we don't know ourselves and as a result our authentic self becomes compromised.

> **Ask yourself these questions:**
> - How much time do I spend being my real self?
> - Am I easily influenced by others?
> - Do I stand up for what I believe in?
> - What prevents me from being myself?
> - How well do I know myself?

Surveys show that people who score higher on tests for authenticity, have a higher self esteem, are generally happier people and are more satisfied with life.

"Your time is limited, so don't waste it living someone else's life. Don't be trapped by dogma – which is living with the results of

other people's thinking. Don't let the noise of others' opinions drown out your own inner voice. And, most importantly, have the courage to follow your heart and intuition. They somehow already know what you truly want to become. Everything else is secondary." – Steve **Jobs**

To be true to yourself means to act in accordance with who you are and what you believe. If you know and love yourself, you will find it effortless to be true to yourself. You cannot be true to anyone else until you are able to be true to yourself. Much the same way you cannot *truly* love another until you are able to love yourself truly. Be who you are and have the courage to accept yourself as you are with the intention to discover your true essence, so you may live as your authentic self.

If you have been living your life in a way to please others, I encourage you to start making the necessary steps today to discover the real you.

Pretending to be someone else for the purpose of being accepted by others is not living your highest truth, and will end up frustrating you in the long run because your choice to be unauthentic is causing an internal battle with yourself, your "true self."

Many young people believe that when they do things to please their peers, such as drink when they don't necessarily want to, or behave in ways that are inappropriate and feel uncomfortable, they will be liked and accepted. Many times they go against their own sense of what feels right and often find them self in a troubled state. I acknowledge that peer pressure is real but I know that standing in your truth is the only place to stand, even if you stand there alone.

When you operate from a place that is not a reflection of your true self, in the long run you end up confused and unhappy. Respect of self comes from being true to self and acting in accordance with the alignment of your true and authentic nature. The way you project yourself is how others will accept you – respect and honor your truth, and others will do the same. What you give to the world the world will give back to you.

Be true to yourself and allow your individuality and uniqueness to shine through. It's appropriate to respect the opinions of others but remember that someone else's opinion of your life, and your truth, really bears no importance on you unless you allow it to. Whilst everyone is entitled to their OWN opinion it does not mean that you have to take their opinion on as your own.

As a teenager I was always unique, and in many cases was not understood by my peers or the adults around me. I had my own mind as they say, but more importantly I was never prepared to do something that was out of alignment with what I felt was right for me.

I remember my father wanting me to go off to college to study Corporate Law. Well let me tell you there was nothing about this professional title that excited or motivated me. However, the condition for me going off to college was that I would have to go into this field of study. Ahhhh no thank you!!

I decided to go straight from high school to the job world and even though I ended up in a job that I really hated, at the time that I took the job I felt that it was something that I wanted to do. Discovering what I did NOT like sent me on a quest to discover what I did like and once I found it, even though others thought I was crazy or had so much more "potential" to do something greater, I knew that I had found what I was called to do at that time… and I LOVED it!

Eventually because what I projected out was love, comfort and peace in what I was doing, others, who had previously questioned it, came to accept it as something that I was meant to do. See how that works? People will receive you the way you present yourself every time and every day. But at the end of the day what is most important is that you are comfortable, happy and at peace within yourself.

Being true to who you authentically are takes courage. It requires you to be introspective, sincere, open-minded and honest. It does not mean that you are inconsiderate or disrespectful of others. It means that you will not let others define you or make the decisions for you that you should be making for yourself.

Be true to the very best that is in you and live your life consistent with *your* highest values and aspirations. Those who are most successful in life have dared to creatively express themselves, and in turn what has happened is they have assisted in broadening the perspectives and experiences of others around them. So see, it's a win-win for everyone!

Tips on Being True to Yourself:

- Be who you are, genuinely.
- Follow your own values and your convictions.
- Listen to the advice of others, but make your own decisions.
- Recognize, appreciate and develop your unique talents.
- Stand up for your own beliefs and you will gain respect.
- Know that it's okay to be 'different', and embracing your uniqueness is your gift to yourself.
- Understand that by being yourself, you are enriching the lives of others around you.

SIX

Do You Like What Life Shows You?

I submit to you today that if the Kingdom of Heaven is within so is hell. Each of us has the power to create our own personal heaven or hell on earth. Your life is what you make it! Your reality is created by your perception which is a combination of your thoughts, your beliefs and your truths.

Your beliefs are your thoughts that you have held for a period of time. Your truths are your beliefs that you have held for a period of time. Thoughts, beliefs and truths are different for different people. Your thoughts, beliefs and truths are the canvas and paints that construct your own life.

One of my all time favorite songs is from the movie Mahogany sung by Diana Ross... "Do you

51

know where you're going to? Do you like the things that life is showing you? Do you know?" I often ask this question of others and the answer that I get most often is "No". The sad thing is that when you don't know who you are, you won't know where you're going. If you don't know where you're going you can't know how to get there and in the interim you hate the process and everything you see around you.

I admit it can become all too easy to focus on those things that are negative, but it is important to understand that everything that we do is ultimately a choice. Feelings of exhaustion, overwhelm, stress, and overworked, when focused on, will create a negative mindset that can creep up on you. The more you focus on these negatives the more they will be a part of your experience.

Research has demonstrated that positive thinking can have a wide variety of benefits from improving your self-confidence, to boosting your physical health. So how can you eliminate negative thoughts and replace them with a more positive outlook?

Even if you are not a natural-born optimist there are things you can do to develop your positive thinking skills and reap the benefits that positive thinking brings. To be successful at this you have to begin the practice of conscious thinking – being conscious of the thoughts you think.

Begin by becoming aware of your thoughts. Being a positive thinker begins with an awareness of the things that you think about. The stream of conscious flow of thought can be difficult to focus on, especially if introspection does not come easy to you. When you encounter a challenging situation try to notice how you think about what is happening. Do you engage in negative self-talk? Do you mentally criticize yourself or others? Negative thinking can present major obstacles but identifying such thoughts is the first step in overcoming them.

Some of the most common types of negative thinking involve focusing on only the undesirable aspects of a situation. For example you were just hired for a job in a position that has been a dream for you for some time, but you have to drive a one hour commute both ways. Despite the good news of the new job, that evening you find yourself focusing more on the drive time, how early you are going to have to get up in the morning, and how much you are going to have to spend on gas rather than focusing on, and being grateful for, the fact that you just landed your dream job. You choose to become more focused on the negative aspects rather than reflect on, and express gratitude for the positive ones.

We become so consumed with the things that we cannot control rather than focusing on the things which we can. I tell my clients all the time that it's important to understand that **we do not**

control everything. For example you do not control whether you wake up in the morning, whether the weather is sunny or rainy, whether someone decides to drive crazily on the highway, or whether your co-worker does, or does not do their job.

We have a tendency to be so concerned about the things over which we have no control, that it completely affects those areas over which we do have control. A very good friend of mine once told me, *"If you can do something about it then do it, if you can't why worry about it?"* That has been very valuable advice to me throughout my life. It helps me to re-center when things around me *seem to be* out of control.

Changing negative thought cycles can be a challenge, and please understand that it is a process that takes time. Positive thinking is not about putting on a pair of rose-colored glasses and ignoring all the negative things around you.

Acknowledging the negative is okay, but allowing it to become your focus only lends to draw more of it to you. Remember energy flows where your thoughts or attention go.

So you may wonder what you should do when you find yourself overwhelmed with negative thoughts. Start with small steps after all you are trying to cultivate a new habit. Changing a behavior, as with keeping a resolution, takes time.

Start by identifying one area of your life that is most affected by negative thinking. This may be your personal appearance or how you relate to, or view, others. By beginning with a single and specific area of your life the changes will be more likely to stick in the long run.

Imagine that you have chosen to focus on your negative thinking with regards to your personal appearance. The next step is to spend a little time each day evaluating your own thoughts about how you look. When you find yourself thinking critical thoughts about yourself take a moment to pause and reflect. While you might be upset that you put on a few pounds, berating yourself about it is not the best approach and won't allow for the weight to come off.

If you don't like the way you look then make a decision to do something about it; incorporate exercise into your daily routine or change your eating habits to incorporate better food choices. This you can control. But say for example, you have put on some extra weight because your doctor prescribed a medication for the improvement of your health, and one of the side effects is weight gain. Well, as long as you have to take the medication you really can't do anything about the extra weight. Rather than focusing on the weight visualize your health improving, which could possibly eliminate the need for the medication.

Watch carefully for negative self-talk. When your inner monologue starts suggesting that you will never get rid of the weight or that trying to get it off is too hard, find a way to take a more positive view of the situation. For example if you feel you are unable to finish your exercise routine forgive yourself. Make a decision that you will do better the following day and focus on finishing the routine tomorrow. Or you might make a decision to modify your routine so you are able to complete it. In any event focus on what you are able to do to bring solution to the situation, rather than perpetuating, focusing on and talking about the problem.

Being a positive thinker is more about taking a proactive approach to your life instead of feeling hopeless, discouraged, overwhelmed or stressed. Positive thinking allows you to tackle life's challenges by looking for effective ways to resolve conflict, and come up with creative solutions to having better experiences.

Your thoughts affect your mental, emotional and physical states, so remember that making an effort to be more positive will be well worth it. This is not a step-by-step process that you can complete and be done with. It takes practice, lots of practice. It involves a lifelong commitment to looking inside yourself and being willing to challenge negative thoughts and make positive changes. It is a way of life.

"We can complain because rose bushes have thorns, or rejoice because thorn bushes have roses." – **Abraham Lincoln**

"*Adversity can be turned into*

Opportunity,

Simply by adjusting

our **Perception**

And our **Attitude.**"

Gail Lynn Goodwin

SEVEN

Perception is Everything

"I will love the light for it shows me the way, yet I will endure the darkness for it shows me the stars." – Og Mandino

The power of perception is very important to understand because it is how and why you attract, and experience, what you attract and experience on a day to day basis. Your perception creates your reality and if you have a sincere desire to begin to consciously and consistently create more desirable outcomes than you are currently experiencing, you must pay attention to this chapter.

Firstly let's ensure that we have a clear understanding of the definition of perception. As defined in the Merriam Webster Dictionary, "perception is the act of perceiving; an observation or mental image: An obsolete consciousness; a quick, acute and intuitive cognition; a capacity for comprehension."

Based on this definition we can conclude that your perception of something is an observation, interpretation or mental image that you hold with regard to some event, condition or circumstance. It is how *you* SEE things in the world around you that molds, shapes and determines your individual perception.

Individual perceptions are formed and based on an "awareness" of the circumstances through physical sensation. This can be a very limited way of viewing life for we reduce and restrict the "bigger picture" to that which we can only physically experience in our limited human awareness and understanding. We often allow our perceptions to be formed based on what we can see, hear, taste, touch and smell. Our perceptions are based on our senses.

In this light we allow ourselves to be limited to judgments when what we SEE around us conflicts with what we desire individually. We judge and label others based on our chosen beliefs and perceptions and tend not to give respect to their beliefs and perceptions.

We have all been given the spiritual right in our gift of "free will" to view and discern what's true, or untrue, in "reality" as we choose. The truth is though that there is so much more "reality" which we limit ourselves to experience by basing everything on our physical senses.

How you have come to perceive, view and see things in the physical world has happened as a result of a belief you established at some point in the past. Many times our perceptions can be flawed or at the very least quite limited, depending on how they were acquired and the evidence we allowed to determine the given conclusion. A common and misguided perception among people who are unconsciously creating their realities, is that you perceive things the way you do because that is the way things are. This is a perceived truth and not a "Higher Truth". Why? Because the "Higher Truth" is that the reason why things are the way they are is because that is how you perceive them to be.

In reality a perception is merely the effect of any given belief. Perception is an individualized awareness based on a belief that you have established. If the belief is flawed or self limiting and based on anything less than a "Higher Truth", the perception that you hold (with regard to the held belief), will be flawed and self limiting also. The experience had as a result of this will correlate precisely with what you "perceive" to be true.

In reality there exists no such thing as an "untruth." However, lower truths and "Higher Truths" do exist and your choice on which of these you choose to believe, makes it *your* truth. This gives it the permission to unfold in your life just as you believe, perceive, accept and expect that it will.

The perceptions that you choose to hold regarding an event, condition or circumstance, will determine the experience that you will encounter. If you believe that it is impossible or you believe that it is possible, you are correct. If you believe that it is good or you believe that it is bad, you are correct. Your willingness to recognize and accept how the power of perception can affect your world, however you choose it to, will provide you with a sense of power and assurance that you alone are the co-creator of your reality. Acceptance of this will help you to step into your power, no longer allowing powerlessness and uncertainty to become, and remain a way of life for you.

Since the beginning of man the greatest and most insightful spiritual teachers have taught this. It has been documented in numerous spiritual texts throughout history, and Science has proven and clearly documented this fact.

Please understand, all that you encounter and experience in your life regardless of how it may appear at the time, ultimately unfolds precisely as you perceive that it will. This awareness will enable you to be more deliberate and intentional in your created experiences.

Unfortunately because many are not aware of this, their perceptions lead them to unpleasant or uncomfortable experiences. However in spite of this discomfort, every experience that comes across our path serves to teach us very valuable lessons that are necessary to learn on our life's journey. It is all designed to bring you back to the path of truth – "Higher Truth."

So what is the "Higher Truth"?

You are a Limitless and Infinite Being existing in an Infinite and Limitless Universe with **the**

ability to experience life in the way that you choose.

The "Higher Truth" is that truth is infinite in nature. Whatever quality of truth you choose that molds, shapes and determines you individually, is drawn from this place of infinite proportion. It is real and tangible in all areas of your life - physical, financial, relational, emotional and spiritual.

By developing this understanding and establishing it as a firm belief, you can fully express heartfelt gratitude for the growth you are experiencing. You will become empowered to begin attracting more outcomes that are pleasing rather than more of what you don't want to experience.

Know that you are empowered, without exception, to be the co-creator of your reality. What life reflects back to you in the form of reality is what you have projected by way of your perceptions. See that ALL things, regardless of how they may appear, are being created by you and that it is all happening for a "greater good" and higher purpose.

By successfully adopting and internalizing this way of thinking you will usher into your experiences a life far more fulfilling than you have ever previously experienced or perceived as being possible. By doing so you will have made a huge step forward in discovering how you can consciously, purposefully and intentionally begin to design your life - a life that you desire, deserve and were created to enjoy.

Many of us are taught things that later in life we discover weren't really the 'truth'. These were perceived truths that even though they may not have been based on "real truth," we adjusted our mental, emotional, physical and spiritual behaviors to..

Let me illustrate how powerful perception is when compared to something that is not really true…Think back to thousands of years ago when people believed that the world was flat. Even though these teachings were not based on the "real truth" they were truth for those that believed it. Although not really true, it was in fact a perceived truth of those that lived during the time of that belief.

Consider the limitations and restrictions that that perceived belief had on the population of that era. They were terrified to venture out too far because they were afraid that they would fall off the edge of the earth! How much did they miss out on because of this belief? How much are you missing out on because you are holding on to perceptions that are not in alignment with the Highest Truth for you? Many things that are perceived to be true, in fact, aren't based on truth at all.

Today your perceptions can be affecting you in the area of your finances. You are experiencing lack, or hardship, because of what you perceive to be true either at a conscious or subconscious level, regarding finances. If you are experiencing poor health conditions it is more than likely due to a perception, or belief, that you hold at some level regarding your health. If you are experiencing anything other than healthy and harmonious relationships it is due to a perceived truth that you hold regarding those relationships, which is not in alignment with your "Highest Truth".

The "real truth" is that you (we) have been created in the image and likeness of the Source/God/Creator and provided with the power and authority to co-create EVERY event, condition, and circumstance in our lives, whether physically, financially, relationally, emotionally or spiritually. The focus and attention that you choose with regard to each of these areas of your life will determine, with absolute and unwavering certainty, how each unfolds.

If you'll look deep enough you will begin to discover many perceptions that you currently hold that are not in alignment with real truth at all. They are perceptions that are held based on traditionally established faulty beliefs that you heard, or were taught, at various times in your life.

Although I do understand that many of the perceptions that you currently hold are the result of the assumed or established beliefs taught to you as a child, and you fully trusted in, and believed, that what was taught to you was true, there comes a time when we must analyze and determine for ourselves whether these perceptions are in alignment with our heartfelt desires and 'knowing'. We should be prepared to question whether they are enabling or hindering, our ability to experience the abundance that is, and always has been, available to us.

At some point, discovering the perceived truths that are blocking your ability to receive and allowing them to be replaced with that which is your "Highest Truth" becomes *your* responsibility, especially if you choose to experience the things that you desire and live the quality of life intended for you – **a life that is limitless.**

What you perceive to be truth makes it "your truth" not the "real truth". The power of perception mirrors your inner world to your outer world and produces results in exact correlation to the perceptions that you choose to hold on to.

Common Held Beliefs about Finances:

- Money is hard to come by.
- You must work hard for money.
- Wealth is only for the fortunate few.
- It takes money to make money.
- Before I can spend it it's gone.
- If I could make more I would have more.

Here is the "Real Truth":

- You were **created in the image and likeness of the Creator,** whatever you perceive that Creator to be.

- You can have anything you desire, **if only you believe.**

- Faith is the **substance** of things hoped for, the **evidence** of things not seen.

- "As a man **thinketh,** so is he."

- We have all been given power to get wealth.

- With God ALL things are possible (which means that **nothing** is impossible.)

"Change the way you look at things, and the things you look at change." – Wayne Dyer

"One new perception,

One fresh thought,

One act of surrender,

One change of heart,

One leap of faith,

Can change your life,

Forever."

Robert Holden

EIGHT

Let It Be

"Let it be, let it be, let it be, let it be, there will be an answer, let it be." – The Beatles

You know what hinders most people from living life freely: Their own inability, or refusal, to just let things be. The only thing that truly exists is the present moment. The past no longer exists and the future does not exist yet most people tend to try to live in those two places of 'existence'.

The biggest obstacle to living life freely is fear. We either fear that things will turn out the way they did before, we fear the thought of it not turning out the way we want it to, or we fear that it will never work out.

"Fear keeps us focused on the past or worried about the future. If we can acknowledge our

fear, we can realize that right now we are okay. Right now, today, we are still alive, and our bodies are working marvelously. Our eyes can still see the beautiful sky. Our ears can still hear the voices of our loved ones." – Thich Nhat Hanh

Many will tell you that they fear the unknown but if you really think about that statement, it's impossible to fear what you don't know. You don't *know* it, so how can you fear it? What people fear is what they **perceive** the unknown to be. The definition or expectation that they attach to it, before they even experience it is what they fear. Fear boils down to three things for people: Not having enough, not doing enough or not being enough.

My personal mantra for myself has become this… **"It is what it is and it will be what it will be!"** This mantra has brought such a source of comfort and ease to my life because in saying it and trusting it, I acknowledge that there are things that I have no control over and that it's okay. One of my favorite quotes is the Serenity Prayer:

"God grant me the serenity to accept the things I cannot change, courage to change the things I can and the wisdom to know the difference."
- Reinhold Niebuhr, Theologian

I remember this prayer hanging up in my father's recording studio when I was a child. I saw and read this prayer a lot because I spent a lot of time at his studio. The profound thing is that even as a child this prayer made a great impact on me. At that time I had no idea that this would be my message to the world. The powerful thing about this realization for me is that we are prepared from the time that we are children, for that which we are called to be and do in the world.

"Truly I tell you, unless you change and become like little children, you will never enter the kingdom of heaven." -Matthew 18:3 KJV

"The kingdom of God cometh not with observation: Neither shall they say, Lo here! Or lo there! For behold, the kingdom of God is within you." – Luke 17:20-21 KJV

See the challenge and frustration comes, because we are looking for our power outside of ourselves. We are looking for the answers outside of ourselves. We are looking for the truth outside of ourselves where it cannot be found because the "real truth" is that all that we seek outside of ourselves can only be found within.

Even as you are reading this book I ask you to process this information not outside of yourself but within. Does it resonate with you deep within your heart and soul? If it does not reject it because on a soul level you know what the truth is for you. We have all been wired with what I call an Internal Guidance System (IGS). It is attached to what we feel. If it "feels" right deep down within then you should always go with it, even if there is a little fear attached to it. However if it does not "feel" right then you should walk away from it. You know how people say, *"if I had only followed my feelings"* or *"I should have followed my heart"*? They usually make this statement when they realize that they made a wrong decision regarding something.

Your "Higher Self" will never lead you wrong. The problem is we have been so encouraged to "listen" to what everyone else says while ignoring what *our self* says. They even tell you that you should not talk to yourself and if you talk to yourself, you absolutely should not answer yourself because then you're crazy. Oh how the world has strategically led us away from ourselves. I am proud to admit that I talk to myself, I answer myself, and I listen to myself. Some of my deepest awareness and understanding has come through this practice. I encourage you to start talking *and* listening to yourself, there are many lessons that come from within.

So how do you practice this? Start by taking time every day to just be silent. Some may call this meditation. I usually recommend taking at least five minutes but if that sounds like a long time to you start with one minute.

First thing in the morning, when I awake, before I get out of bed I check in to see what *myself* wants to say to me today. This might sound silly but I promise you it works. The more you do this you will find you are able to do it for longer periods of time. Make it a goal to increase this time to twenty minutes a day. My personal routine is to do this both in the morning when I awake and at night right before I go to sleep.

Society feels a need to label things as "good" or "bad", "right" or "wrong", "high" or "low", but my personal position at this point in my life is things just are. I try not to use labels but just accept. This has been a major contributor to my experiencing peace in my life even in the midst of "storms". There's a scripture in Romans 14:19, that tells us to, "Pursue the things that make for peace." For me this means that peace is something that you have to go after; the experience of peace comes when we make a decision to experience it by doing what is necessary to acquire it.

With peace comes happiness. They both are the result of living in harmony with our own intuition of truth. We have been created in such a way that when we live true and we live purpose we know it because the reinforcing result called joy, is ours.

At the highest level of your awareness you know what is best for you, what is accessible to you and how to access it. Just as a computer comes equipped with all of the necessary programming to function, so have you been equipped with all that is necessary to function, succeed and create what is necessary for your life's journey. Let it go and let it flow!

Live for today

because Yesterday

has been and gone,

and Tomorrow

may never come.

NINE

Let's Start Over, Make That Change

"Life is like a box of chocolates, but you get to choose which ones you want to eat." – Forest Gump/Denika Carothers

I clearly remember those chocolates that everyone gave out on Valentine's Day when I was in high school. They came in a heart shaped box, were assorted, cheap and very few of them tasted good. There were maybe two specific ones that I liked and would eat. The rest of them I would give to others who weren't as picky as me or I would throw them away.

Even the more expensive boxes of chocolates contained chocolates in them that I would not eat because I did not like the way they tasted. I specifically remember the ones with white filling!

Yuck, I didn't like those. And the ones with the dark liquid cream that tasted like coffee… I didn't eat those either.

I have always been a very selective eater. I knew what I liked and I discovered very quickly what I did not like. However what I came to appreciate as I got older was that certain foods that were prepared for me when I was younger that I did not like the taste of, I ended up liking very much when I began to prepare them for myself and in alignment with *my* tastes.

One such food is oatmeal. My memory recalls my father preparing oatmeal for me as a child and I would always refuse to eat it. There was an occasion when he made a decision that I was going to eat that oatmeal and I made a decision that I was NOT going to eat it. I hated the way his oatmeal tasted and I'm not quite sure exactly how he prepared it, but to me it tasted awful. He decided that I was not going to leave the table until

I ate the oatmeal and I decided that I would stay at that table for the rest of my life *before* I ate that oatmeal.

Well obviously seeing that I am no longer at that table he eventually let me leave, however my freedom did not come because I ate the oatmeal. I was a stubborn little girl who knew what she didn't like and was willing to stand my ground even if it resulted in my behind coming into contact with his belt. Today I love oatmeal but I can tell you that whatever it was that he put in his I do not put in mine!

Even though my truth as a child was that oatmeal tasted bad and I hated it, when I was able to prepare it for myself to my liking and taste, I discovered that it was something that I do like. My relationship with oatmeal had a new start and my truth about oatmeal changed.

Just as I had a new start with oatmeal you can start over in any area of your life in which you choose to. You may have held something as true for most of your life but have reached a point in your life where you aren't sure that what you thought to be true or right is actually true or right, that your belief systems no longer align with the calling of your soul, it's perfectly fine to change your mind and start over. Yes it IS that simple.

So many people hold on to ideas, beliefs and truths until the day they die, unwilling to change, or even entertain the thought of change. Even though they may not be completely convinced within themselves that it is true, they would rather die than admit that they were not living in alignment with their "Highest Truth." Instead of feeling a need **to be right** how about if we just BE and give ourselves permission to be okay with that?

"The secret of change is to focus all of your energy, not on fighting the old, but on building the new." - **Socrates**

Change is something most people resist because the truth is that change can be scary. Even though we might not be happy with our current situation, our rationale is that at least we know how to handle it, because it's something we're used to. Change is a risk that we need to be willing to take to better ourselves and our lives. The first step towards change is being willing to make an effort to control your fear.

So how do you control fear? By acknowledging that what we are afraid of is not real; it does not exist. Our fears are projected thoughts and ideas of what we *believe* will happen. It hasn't happened so how can it be real? Hmmm that was good… Mental check, I will have to remember that one for myself!

Zen practitioners cultivate the "don't know" mind. They work to assume they don't know anything and in that, they are able to see the world with a fresh perspective. This is a great way to approach change – it's an opportunity to start anew and consider all possibilities that can lead to the discovery of new ideas, new thoughts, and new experiences.

Expect without expectations. When we do this we are allowing ourselves to not be attached to how our desires will manifest, we just **expect** them to show up. Say for example you want to take a trip to Australia but your expectation is that the only way you can do this is if you save enough money to buy the ticket yourself. Well suppose the Universe wants to send you a free ticket to Australia by way of a sweepstakes that you feel drawn to enter. Your trip showed up but not according to your expectation. When we open ourselves up to just being and allow 'flow' to take place in our lives, we open ourselves up to the beauty of life being able to show up via many different channels.

What I have found in my own personal process is that when I have an expectation as to how something will show up what I actually do is close myself off to the greater possibilities. Hence I have learned to expect *without* an expectation of how it will manifest. I always experience what I desire but not necessarily in the way that I thought it may have shown up. But hey, what matters most is that it shows up right?

I have learned that change can happen quickly and at any point. Embracing, and being open to change, enables you to flow in what is, rather than approach change from a place of fear and resistance. Every experience in life brings with it very specific lessons and insights. Embracing change opens you up to understanding what these insights and lessons are. Even though circumstances may not turn out the way you want, that's perfectly okay. Believe that they turn out the way that they should. Embracing it can help you deal effectively with what "is" and make any shifts necessary to help you move forward.

Remember *life* is all about change. Things around us are changing all the time even though we may not see or be aware of the changes. For example the house that you leave in the day to go to your job is not the same exact house that you return to. The atmospheric pressure or the temperature in the air may have changed; there may be dust where there was not dust when you left. If you have animals, there may be more fur on the floor than was there before you left home, or the house may smell different if they decided to leave something other than fur on the floor. The foundation may have shifted slightly, while you were gone. There may be less or more leaves on the trees outside of your home. Things are always changing. Learning how to flow rather than resist, helps us to be okay and accepting of what life wants to do. Life just is. And guess what… some parts of life you will never have control over.

Change can be your greatest teacher but only if you give yourself permission to learn from it. As you make a choice to embrace the changes that show up in your life, you give yourself permission to start over. Embracing change can usher in a tremendous amount of peace, calm and courage. When life fails to shake you up with its twists and turns you realize that changes can't break you. You reach a new level of understanding of life, which some might call wisdom. Instead of making change the enemy allow it to be the teacher.

Rather than letting change *affect* you negatively, why don't you just effect change? Sounds good to me: Ding!

"Change is Inevitable, Progress is Optional"

Tony Robbins

TEN

So What! Who Cares?

So congratulations! Now that you have decided that you are ready to start over and make the necessary changes, you're about to make some people around you very uncomfortable. You see not everybody is ready for the changes you are about to make, but so what! Who cares? What is most important is that you do what you need to do for yourself. This is *your* life journey and not everyone will be able to walk it with you.

I tell clients all the time, when you lay down at night even though you may be laying next to someone else, you are essentially lying down with you. Whatever transpired during the day either sits well, or doesn't sit well with you, only you! Nobody else is really affected by your internal life and most people don't care about it either. For the most part everyone around you only cares about themselves. So now it's time for you to do the same and care about the number one person in your life – you! (Okay I hear you… God is the number one person in your life, but God is not a person. So let's put you in the number one *person* spot)

The world has gotten it twisted and they love to tell you how selfish you are being when you decide to look out for yourself. But let me ask you this… if you don't learn how to look out for yourself then essentially who do you expect to look out for you? And will that expectation be met?

Trust me I have learned the importance of looking out for myself, taking time for myself, and putting importance in myself – the things I need, the things I desire and the things that only I can do. The ancient texts tell us, "Love your neighbor as yourself." The truth is if I don't have it for me, I can't give it to you. If you don't give it to you, you can't genuinely give it to someone else. Now, if you don't align with this as your truth that's perfectly okay but this is MY truth.

When I was raising my children, they got to a certain age where I made a decision that their **needs** would come before my wants, but their wants, would not come before mine. In other words, I did not put me on the back burner for my children. I realized as a single mother raising three children on my own, that if I didn't look out for me and give to myself the things that I needed then eventually, I would not be of much use to them.

Mothers have an innate tendency that drives them towards putting everyone else before themselves, but what I discovered, and if you are a mother you might have discovered this too, is when you deny yourself in an effort to be, give and do for everyone else, you can end up becoming very resentful – resentful towards other people or resentful towards life. Resentment breeds anger and anger breeds contempt. Eventually you find that you have turned into a very unhappy, angry or depressed person.

Now please do not get me wrong. I am not suggesting that you do not do for your children. If your children are in need, as a mother or parent, you are responsible to provide for the needs of your children, especially when they are young. What I am doing is encouraging you to put importance and priority into yourself even if that means that what you want, takes priority over what someone else wants: That you get what you want even if they don't.

I have had clients, specifically clients who were mothers and wives, who have complained that they have dedicated their life, and catered to every need and want of their children and their husband, denying themselves in many instances, only to be mistreated and taken for granted in the end. This resulted in them becoming very resentful, regretful, and feeling unfulfilled and empty inside. The children grow up and leave home, and sometimes the husband does too, and then they find that they don't know who they are, what they want, or how to live their lives on their own terms without the responsibility of "having to do for someone else."

I have learned to live my life in such a way that I would not have regrets. This is why I practice mindfulness and being very intentional about what I do, or don't do. It is also very important for me, to know exactly *why* I do what I do. I ask myself the question, *"Am I doing this because it is what I want to do, or am I doing this to please someone else and not walking in accordance with my 'Highest Truth'?"* I have become okay with saying "no" and I have learned to say "no" when it is necessary.

"When you say yes to others, make sure you are not saying no to yourself."– Paulo Cohelho

Treat yourself kindly, that way you won't be waiting for someone else to be kind to you. Make yourself a priority, that way you won't be waiting for someone else to make you feel important. Love yourself, that way when you experience love outside of yourself, you know how to appreciate it, because you know how to give it to yourself as well as give it to that, or them, which are outside of you.

Embrace the reality that this is your life and your journey, and you absolutely have the right to live it in accordance with your "Highest Truth", your desires, and with what you decide is good for you.

Have you ever done something for someone else that not only did you not want to do, but you did not feel good doing it? Well let's erase that habit from the story of your life. Decide from this day forward that you are going to do you and you are going to be okay with that, even if you don't always understand it. What matters most is that when you lay down at night with yourself, you can feel good about what you did that day for you, even if it was staying in bed all day in pajamas and not taking a bath! You may be stinky but at least you'll be happy!

Live your life fully

Love yourself deeply

Laugh at yourself often

Denika Carothers

ELEVEN

Design Your Life Intentionally

When you begin to understand that you have the power to design your life, it empowers you to no longer accept whatever "comes your way". You can set your own intentions with regards to what you want, and don't want to experience in your life. The intention is the creative power that fulfills all of our needs... whether for love, relationships, spiritual awakening, or money. Everything that happens in existence begins with intention. For those of you who believe that you don't have the power or the know-how to create your own life, take a look at this list. It will show you how to design your life INTENTIONALLY!

Examine yourself. Know who you are and what you are able to do. Get a strong handle on your passions, talents, abilities, and weaknesses. Give precious time and energy to this endeavor. It is one of the most valuable things you can do. When asked the question, "Who are you?" you should be able to answer with confidence and certainty. You have to know who you are to know where you are going.

Know why. Know why you want what you want. Know why you do what you do. Knowing your why is the most important start to setting intentions. When you know why you're doing what you're doing you will be driven to press on and press forward, even in the midst of obstacles.

Define your purpose. Identify what you want your life to communicate and contribute. Find your passion and purpose, and you will feel empowered you to live for that which is bigger than you. Write this down. Think about it all the time. Identifying your purpose brings new meaning to your life. It moves you from living only for yourself, to being concerned with how your living can make the lives of others better.

Pay attention to how you think. Your thoughts become your words and your words create your reality. When a thought presents itself in your mind take a moment to tap in to whether this thought is in alignment with what you desire to experience.

Get in to the breath space. Between your thought and your reaction, is a space that I call the "breath space." It is a place in which to pause and breathe before you react. This is a state of pure awareness. This is the ideal state in which to plant your intentions.

Remain centered. Intention is more powerful when it comes from a place of contentment, rather than a place of anxiety, desperation, lack or need. In the creative or designing process it is important to stay centered, and refuse to be influenced by your doubts or criticisms, or the doubts and criticisms of other people.

Remain open to the process. Expect without attaching expectations to the outcome. The most powerful way to design your life intentionally is to be open to the process and detached from the results. When you are able to detach from the expectation of the end result you open yourself up to the flow.

Release, rather than resist. After you set an intention let it go. Simply stop thinking about it, and if it comes into your thinking hold it with love and gratitude, and release it again. Release the attachment to a specific result and live in the wisdom of the unseen, by faith.

Detach from the outcome. Attachment is based on fear and insecurity, while detachment is based on the unquestioning belief in the power of your "true" and "Higher Self." Set the intention for everything to work out as it should then let go and allow for the openings that will bring the opportunities your way.

Have Faith. Your "Higher Self", your intuitive force, knows that everything is, and will be, alright. Remember that everything is perfect in every moment. If you believe it is possible let your belief translate into the possible being made manifest. See it, feel it, smell it, and taste it daily. Faith is the fertilizer for intention.

Let God/Source/Spirit/The Universe handle the details. "If it don't fit, don't force it, just relax and let it go." (Kellee Patterson) Being able to surrender to Divine design is the most effective way to design our lives by intention. Surrendering to the Divine is essentially surrendering to the knowledge that all that is, is, and there are some things that we will just never have control over. Designing your life with this knowledge always produces 'better than you could have even imagined'.

Be free to live life as you choose. Know that your life is your own and while others may have many opinions, suggestions, or advice about how you should live it, the one that ultimately gets to make that decision is you. It is important to be okay with however you decide to do that. Remember that others will always accept us the way we present ourselves. If you are insecure in your beliefs, others will question you. If you are confident in your approach, others will receive you confidently.

Keep it simple. As crazy as this may sound living a simple life requires a great deal of intention. We are surrounded by hectic, crazy, busy, hurried and complicated… we live in a world where simplicity is shunned upon and complication is glorified. And the funny thing is, that complicated can never feel as liberating as simple.

"The essence of life is not in the great victories and grand failures, but in the simple joys." - Jonathan Lockwood Huie

Let the past go. Don't let the circumstances of your past negatively determine the pattern of your future life. Always take accountability for your choices and move on. You do not need to be stuck in old patterns of living. Embrace every morning as a new opportunity.

Don't compare yourself to others. You were born to live *your* life. There is no sense wasting your life being concerned about what others are doing in their lives. They have the right to live their life and you have the right to live yours. You were *born* to live your life – determine to be good at it. After all this life is the only shot you have to live it.

Learn from others. I have learned that successful people are curious people. They possess the humility to learn from others. Identify people who are accomplishing your desires and goals. Study them and learn from them. Identify the person who most looks like what you believe you are and plug into their wisdom and knowledge.

Question yourself. Ask yourself the hard questions that you might not necessarily appreciate others asking you. When you question yourself you come to understand the inner workings of the way you think, what motivates you, what frustrates you, what serves you and what you may need to let go of. Do not be afraid to *answer* your questions either.

Don't be afraid to acknowledge your fears. Contrary to acceptance, your fears come to serve very intentional purposes. Humans have fears, which are usually motivated by one of three things – not having enough, not doing enough or not being enough. Remember that everyone confronts some type of fear. Acknowledging our fears and being willing to question them releases their power over us.

Visualize regularly. Make it a daily practice to see yourself living the life you want to design. Where are you? Who are you with? What are you doing? How does it feel? By doing this practice you come to realize that your ideal life is actually more achievable than you might have originally thought. The power of visualization has been instrumental in turning dreams into reality.

Take time and count to 10 (minutes). Spending quality time with your own self for introspection, reflection, and meditation is very powerful. My advice to clients is invest the first 10 minutes of your day in yourself. The first minutes of your day should belong to only you, even if you have to wake up earlier to accomplish this. Upon waking up think about the day ahead and what you want from it – what do you want to feel and what do you want to achieve? Remember the first few minutes after waking are the most crucial in setting the tone and mood for the entire day.

Listen to your inner voice. Some call it intuition; others call it instinct. I call it my IGS, my Internal Guidance System, or "Higher Self." Those who live their lives with purpose, tune into this voice regularly through whatever means works for them. Some achieve this through prayer, some through meditation, while others through stillness, or connecting with nature outdoors. Know that your heart knows all things. When we betray it or tune it out, things usually don't go too well. This voice cannot be silenced even though we may choose not to pay attention to it. If you pay attention to it and follow its direction, your life will transform.

Be aware of your energy and how you direct it. I am a huge energy person. I believe that everything is energy, energy is everything, and it is important to pay attention to how it is directed. It's no different than the powerful energy that runs through an electricity line. If directed correctly it is beneficial and powerful, if misdirected it can be destructive and explosive. Energy is currency. Invest it where it matters most.

"Know when to hold em, know when to fold em, know when to walk away and know when to run." – ***Kenny Rodgers.*** I am a huge proponent of eliminating what no longer serves you in your life. This pertains to people, places and things! Often we are hell bent on holding on to what no longer serves us whether it be people, things, jobs or habits, because we feel a sense of obligation to do so. Choose to be in places that motivate, uplift and empower you. Choose people to be in your circle who are supportive, inspiring and loving. Get around people who are giving, encouraging, and show themselves friendly. Remember everyone that you are a friend to will not be a friend to you. *You* are responsible for the energy you allow into your space. Give yourself permission to disconnect from others with love if need be. Remember… some come for a reason, some for a season and very few will be in your life for a lifetime. Learn to know which is which.

Do what makes you happy. Choose to do only that which makes you happy. If you don't align with doing something, don't do it. Be true to yourself and walk in who you authentically are. We live in a society where everyone feels a need, or a right, to control the actions and thoughts of others. But you know what makes you happy and more importantly, you know what does not. Don't give your valuable energy, time or attention to anything that does not return value to you. Remember you are responsible for your own actions. No one can "make" you do anything. Walk in your own power… in this you will always feel powerful.

Keep it real! Don't fake it till you make it! That quote absolutely irritates me! (Let me get back into my Zen space… woosah!). I don't even want to know where it originated. Anything that is fake will NEVER be real... I don't care how you spin it. Marvin Gaye and Tammi Terrell sing it best... "Ain't nothin' like the REAL thing baby!" So when you set out to design your life intentionally be sure to keep it real, authentic and truthful. When you do this you will always be true to yourself and to others. Remember what you give to the world, the world returns back to you... **so keep it real!**

Design your Life by your Intention Not by someone else's Suggestion.

Denika Carothers

ABOUT THE AUTHOR

A native from the island of the Bahamas, Denika Carothers, a Mindset Transformation Coach and Parenting Expert, specializes in helping women, young and old, transform their mindset from one of conflict and limitation, to one that is empowering and liberating. What sets her apart from her competition is her spiritual insight, and nderstanding of how to build successful relationships through soulful connections.

Her platform, C.H.A.N.G.E. – The Catalyst for Success, is designed to invigorate, inspire and provoke her audience to give themselves permission to step out of what is not working, know that you CAN have whatever you desire and how to live in the power of your authentic and your truth. Her gift of insight enables her to tap into the heart and soul of others and help them to identify the self-created barriers that cause emotional, mental and even spiritual conflicts.

Her inspirational and life changing perspective, which she arrived at by conquering her own life challenges, offers her clients and audiences a transformational view of how to 'GROW' through it all. Her clients and colleagues say that she is the "bridge between your questions and your answers."

A Transformation Agent at heart, she empowers and inspires others through Speaking, Coaching, Mentoring and Authorship. Her mission is to "Give Love a Voice to Change the World One Thought at a Time."

So What Do You Think?

If you enjoyed Who In the Hell Do You Think You Are, would you mind taking a minute to write a review on Amazon. Even a short review helps, and it would mean a lot to me.

If someone you care about is struggling with the life that they are currently experiencing, and you would like to help them to live a victorious life, please send him or her, a copy of this book.

If you'd like to order copies of this book for your company, school or group of friends, please go to www.DenikaCarothers.com/who-in-the-hell-do-you-think-you-are.

Finally, if you'd like to get free bonus materials from this book and receive updates on my future projects, you can sign up for my newsletter at DenikaCarothers.com.

Your life is created by your thoughts. Choose good thoughts!!

For more information about Denika Carothers visit:

www.DenikaCarothers.com

www.facebook.com/denika.penncarothers

www.facebook.com/livewithpurposetoday

www.twitter.com/denikacarothers

www.linkedin.com/pub/denika-carothers

Always End the Day With a

Positive Thought.

No Matter How

Hard Things Were,

Tomorrow's a Fresh

Opportunity To

Make it Better.

Notes

Unless otherwise indicated, all Scripture quotations are from the King James Version of the Bible.

1.   As A Man Thinketh
1. Panache Desai, Spiritual Teacher
2. Dr. Wayne Dyer, "Change Your Thoughts, Change Your Life"
3. The Bible, KJV
4. www.happinessinyourlife.com

2.   Get Out Of Your Head
1. www.merckmanuals.com
2. www.en.wikipedia.org/wiki/heart-development
3. www.pennmedicine.org
4. Dr. Wayne Dyer
5. Origins of our Thoughts, K. Ferlic 2009
6. Leonardo DeVinci www.brainyquote.com

3.   What You Focus On Expands
1. James Redfield, Celestine Vision
2. Dan Millman, The Life You Were Born to Live
3. Maya Angelou, www.oprah.com
4. Napoleon Hill, Think and Grow Rich
5. Opray Winfrey, www.africanamericanquotes.org /Oprah-winfrey

4. The Man In The Mirror

1. Edward De Bono, www.shinyquote.com
2. Dove Real Beauty, www.realbeautysketches.cove.us
3. Renee Englen,
   www.psychology.northwestern.edu/engeln-cv
4. Albert Einstein, www.en.wikiquote.org

5. To Thine Own Self Be True

1. Steve Jobs, www.news.stanford.edu,
   Commencement address (2005)

6. Do You Like What Life Shows You?

1. Diana Ross, Mahogany 1976
2. Kendra Cherry, Psychology Expert
   www.psychology.about.com
3. Abraham Lincoln, www.site2quotes.com
4. Gail Lynn Goodwin, www.inspiremetoday.com

7. Perception is Everything

1. Og Mandino, Greatest Secrets to Success 1990
2. Merriam Webster Dictionary
3. www.psychologytoday.com
4. www.themindunleashed.org
5. Dr. Wayne Dyer, Success Secrets
6. Robert Holden, www.robertholden.org

8. Let It Be

1. The Beatles, Let It Be 1970
2. Thich Nhat Hanh, Fear: Essential Wisdom For
   Getting Through the Storm

3. Reinhold Niebuhr, The Serenity Prayer, www.en.wikipedia.org
4. The Bible

9. Let's Start Over, Make That Change

1. Forest Gump, 1994
2. Socrates, www.en.wikiquote.org
3. Colleen M. Busch, Fire Monks: Zen Mind Meets Wildfire
4. Tony Robbins

10. So What! Who Cares?

1. Paulo Cohelho, www.motivationalreads.com

11. Design Your Life Intentionally

1. Jonathan Lockwood Huie, www.followingmyjoy.com
2. Kenny Rogers, Album:The Gambler 1978
3. Marvin Gay & Tammi Terrell, Album: You're All I Need 1968

NOTES

NOTES

NOTES

.

www.ingramcontent.com/pod-product-compliance
Lightning Source LLC
LaVergne TN
LVHW021346080426
835508LV00020B/2138